abdulla pashew

DICTIONARY

OF

MIDNIGHT

translated from the kurdish by
alana marie levinson-labrosse

PHONEME
MEDIA

Phoneme Media
P.O. BOX 411272
Los Angeles, CA 90041

ISBN: 978-1-944700-80-5
Library of Congress Control Number forthcoming

This book is distributed by Publishers Group West

Cover design and typesetting by Jaya Nicely
Cover art by Ismael Khayat

Printed in the United States of America

Phoneme Media is a nonprofit media company dedicated to
promoting cross-cultural understanding, connecting people
and ideas through translated books and films.

http://phonememedia.org

DICTIONARY

OF

MIDNIGHT

For a Green Girl

From a distance, you heard my name.
Naive, you loved me.
They say you lived among my poems.
Night after night
they gave you sweet chills.

You don't know me.
Believe me, you don't.
The world you desire
I can never give you.
My world is all sadness.
Joys are few.
My palace is ruins:
a shelter only for books and poems.
The one my heart and eyes face in prayer
is no more than a shattered idol.

Stay away from me,
from my life,
from my bleak eyes.
Stay away from me, from my poems,
these bouquets
I arrange for a queen of bouquets.

28.10.1968
Hawler

Twelve Lessons for Children

I.

Children,
rebels,
Those for whom life is a bitter rival,
when tomorrow you grow up
in our folksongs,
in lauks and hayrans,
in our novels,
in the poetry of a coward poet,
you may often hear
about our struggle for freedom,
about our bravery,
but never believe a word,
they tell lies,
pure lies!

II.

Children,
nowhere claims our hundreds of paths.
Our memory's lamp is so weak
we take blind steps.

Children,
legend says,
once upon a time,
in a land, there was a tribe
whose champion
was blind.
He took aim at the air.
Their philosopher
was a fortune teller
who nightly read the signs

so he would know when his enemy
was going to knot a rope around his neck.
Their wise man
was deaf and dumb,
his short patience spanning 1,000 years.
The miserable tribe
counted the nights,
counted the days,
eating bread and applause three times a day,
waiting for the enemy
to knot a rope around their own neck.

III.

Children,
it is you who must shake the muted brook,
you are the earthquake
who tomorrow must rupture the sleeping headwaters.
It is you who tomorrow
must break the handmade boundary,
reforge the broken links
in the chain:
it is you, tomorrow,
from Qamishli,
from the Diyarbakir of Skeikh Saeed,
from wounded Sulaimani,
from Mahabad of Qathi,
under one principle, meet
and understand:
he who will be Kurdish in the new generation
must carry within his baggage
the path to unify the Kurds.

IV.

Children,
in yesterday's lessons,

I said, "Since creation, we
have lied to ourselves
in our daily lives,
our actions, our writing:
we are without philosophy."
I said this and the world collapsed.
The cloud of accusation
moved toward my thought's horizon.

Children,
for God's sake ask them,
ask the ones whose eyes
don't even see their feet,
don't be afraid, ask, say,
"From journeys through straits made of blood,
for children, what have you brought?
Tell us, what have you brought?'

   V.

Children,
those for whom life is a bitter rival,
over the course of history, the mothers of this country,
their breasts
have lacked the milk of freedom.
Throughout history, the mountains of this country
have lacked a prophet.

Children,
in the embers of your eyes,
I am waiting for a Zarathustra
to come, to displace the idols.
I am waiting for
the thunder of an Avesta
to come, to crack open the liver of darkness.

VI.

Children!
I searched the fortress of the mountains,
I heard the bullet casings
discussing, inside an empty fortress,
the martyred Peshmerga.

VII.

Children!
My intended is a pigeon in Diyarbakir.
She likes mountains, partridge song, and the color of snow.
To marry her,
link by link, I cut across the mountain chain.
Page by page, I tore my calendar.

My passport
was hope and a smile, it was
a pot of kohl and a fistful of henna.
When I knocked at the border's door,
instead of a kiss,
the warm kiss of my intended,
yellow spit and a black boot
soiled my forehead.

VIII.

Children,
those for whom life is a bitter rival,
on the oily chest of Baba Gurgur,[1]
near the silver cascade of inverse flames,
I saw a small tomb
on which was written:
Here a bright-eyed, Kurdish child
died of hunger.

---

[1] Baba Gurgur, situated near the contested city of Kirkuk, is considered one of the largest
oil fields in the world. Its eternal flames, a result of natural gas emissions, are said to be
Nebuchadnezzar's fiery furnace.

IX.

Children,
he who sows a grain of wheat
reaps an ear.
He who sheds a drop of blood
paints a tableau.
He who but looses a shout from his mouth
hears such echoes of his own voice.
But we
who have sown skulls and eyes
and watered them with blood,
cannot see our harvest:
    not a single ear of wheat ripens.

Children,
let us shift the stream's course,
the stream that carries our blood,
let us renew that soil
that swallows skulls and eyes.
Then, I will show you fields of light.
Then, I will harness the harvest to your will.

X.

Children,
on the yellow foreheads of newspapers,
on the oil pipelines,
in mosques, on the bathroom walls,
ten million times
we wrote, "Long live the oppressed!"
We wrote, "Long live the workers!"
But not even once
could all our writing
become the bread
to fill the stomach of one worker.

XI.

Children,
those for whom life is a bitter rival,
at night, in my dreams, I traveled.
I went to great hall of the U.N.
As the gate swallowed me,
I saw a black man who held his own flag,
a white man who held his own flag.
Every man I saw held his own flag.
They shouted:
Stateless, get out.
Flagless, get out.
I replied,
No need to shout.
When I return,
I will tell the children this story.

XII.

Children,
if you read my lessons
by day,
huddle in the corner.
If by night,
let the light be low.
I know very well:
if your elders discover what you're reading
they will brand you
and burn my lessons
and hang Hallaj's corpse[2]
all over again.

1970-1971
Kurdistan

---

[2] Mansur Al-Hallaj (858-922), a prominent Sufi, was executed by the Abbasid Caliph Al-Muqtadir for such revolutionary statements as, "Ana al Haqq," or, "I am the Truth." What was to him a statement of unity with the divine was to the Caliph a heretical claim of divinity.

A Winter Image

Tonight, I touched
the dictionary of midnight.
Its words ran from me
like ants.

The child I saw in the evening
shaded by the mosque's wall
who had cloaked himself in hunger,
who attacked God, a scarecrow,
is my guest tonight.
He has made a bed of my ceiling,
wiping the stars
from the sky with his fragile fingers,
blocking the skylight,
keeping the loose hair of the moon
from tumbling down.

My little guest,
why do you strike out?
What do you want from me?
Come down!
At dawn,
I will unwind the knotted way,
I will break the coffer of the skyline
and fetch for you the golden loaf.

Come down.
Do not slaughter the stars,
do not slam against the skylight.
Be patient.
I will set fire to the slogans on the city's arches,
I will set fire to the fingers of cowardly poets,
the chairs and tables in

every room of every terrible mansion.
At dawn,
I won't forget.
I will unwind the knotted way,
I will break the coffer of the skyline
and fetch for you the golden loaf.
Come down.
Do not slaughter the stars,
Do not slam against the skylight,
my little guest,
come down.

9.11.1972
Kurdistan: Gelyawa Village

A Letter Abroad

Borders swallow my voice.
The road to the printing press
travels through the red pen.
Jokers
have locked all the doors
and laid crimson rugs
under my silence.
My last poem,
since it was born,
sleeps on the green twig
of my tongue,
like a squirrel.

I have written to you.
I have written some slim lines to you.
I have written some poems,
like fallen fledglings.
But so what?
I can't find a post office
that will deliver our letters.
I can't find a single newspaper
from the lines of which
kisses rise and open their eyes.

I call to you, lovers,
I call to you,
be ready.
Let's hold our own congress.
Let's resolve
to establish our own post office
that will deliver our letters,

to build our own printing press
from the bed of which
kisses will rise and open their eyes.

30.12.1970
Hawler

Two Prefaces
for a Poem Not Yet Written

Don't be angered by the smoke of my words:
the smoke is a weary swallow
that flees the nest in flames.

Don't be angered by the cyclone of my words:
the cyclone
is only a shepherd
that drives the flock
of wayward clouds
to the mountains.

20.1.1973
Hawler

I Cannot Write

I cannot write.
If not with my own blood, I cannot write.
Hone your spears,
sharpen your daggers,
carpet my body with wounds.
I am used to
making ink from my own blood.

1.6.1973
Khalis

To Poets

I

If a word
can't become a bullet
for the rifle of the freedom fighter,
if a word
can't become a winged water bladder
or winged bread
to fly from trench to trench,
then it might as well
become a brush to polish the invader's boots.

II

I am in love with a woman
who doesn't speak the languages of ghosts and jinn.
Like a child, she writes me simple letters.
Like a child, she gazes at me.

III

I never let mist
fall on my city
so that at least
my love will see me.

IV

I am simple,
yes, simple,
and I will remain simple
like the name of my homeland.
The abaya that
yesterday I slipped from my lover's shoulders
will never veil my poetry.

18.7.1973
Kurdistan

If You Come, Come Alone

If you come, come alone.
I resent the rain
when it comes with winds.
I resent the wheat flower
when it twines
its fingers with rust.

Oh, rain in the year of drought,
if you come, come alone,
without wind, without sound.
Oh, gilded wheat flower,
if you come, come without rust.

If you come, come alone
as you are in my heart.
My pillow is for two:
I have two parched chairs,
two cups for tea.

When you come to me alone,
the mountains' ridge
becomes a mother's breast.
The mountains
open my mournful door
to kiss and caress
my outcast forehead.

11.9.1973
Voronezh

Coup d'Etat

Before I knew you,
I was self-centered, a child.
I thought
the wide sky was a tent
set up just for me,
the Earth was an island the floods left behind
to be inhabited by no one but me.

All of a sudden your love arrived
and devastated my citadel, its walls,
altered all colors
and upended all laws.
It turned the vast world into a cage
for my solitude.
It taught me to be content
with half the pillow.

1.12.1973
Voronezh

They Drove Me Out

They drove me out
because my poetry
like a defiant child
threw pebbles
at the leaders' glass palaces.

They drove me out
because my poetry
crossed the red line and
shone a brilliant light
on stolen treasures.

8.12.1973
Voronezh

To the Tycoons

I

You dream of Rasputin's nights,
Croesus' treasure,
and Napoleon's throne,
the spoils of war,
an epic love affair.
I, here,
in the heart of my hovel,
     I dream of
a golden haired child on the horizon,
a fireplace and embers,
a tree abundant with new leaves,
a corner of a free cave.
     I dream.

II

The latest news:
I will go mad
and, mad,
at the peak of your celebrations,
I will inject the corpse of the truth
and resurrect it
from the deathbed of your applause.

The latest news:
I will go mad
and, mad,
in the city square,
I will play with your lies
as children do with marbles.

1973
Hawler

Quatrain

If white hair is sorrow's sign,
the sign of slavery, hunger, and oppression,
then, my friend, when I was born, I shouldn't have had
a single thread of black hair.

1973
Kurdistan

A Match

The news agencies have announced
a soccer match.
The teams: the Kremlin and the White House.
The ball: the skull of a Kurd.
The goal: Kurdistan.
The spectators: the world, silent as the grave.

11.3.1974
Moscow

A Few Lines
About My Age

When Valia asked me,
"When did you first set foot in the world?,"
my laugh, like a rhubarb shoot,
sprouted through the snow of my lips.
My laugh is a cry
that crumples the world's joy.

Yes, Valia,
I was Neanderthal
when I first set foot in this world.
With my own eyes,
I have witnessed the eras of every prophet.
History's shameful convoy
has passed over the creases of my forehead.
And yet,
the underhanded institutions
of this age's corrupt conscience
have not recorded my name
in the book of the living.

19.10.1974
Moscow

A Few Words
About My Heart

This heart of mine
is a train
that has a thousand and one stations.
At each, it stops.
Passengers get off.
Passengers rush on, shoving.

But one passenger, always forlorn,
never disembarks
in any corner of this world.
This passenger is looking for his own name.
This passenger is looking for the pupil of his own eyes.
This passenger is my perpetual wound.
This passenger is my laughter and tears.
This passenger is Kurdistan,
the cradle of my first love.

22.11.1974
Moscow

Poetry

From day to day, more and more, I love poetry.
She is alluring, but timid.
Each day,
we set the time and place of our tryst,
but she rarely arrives, if ever.

16.2.1975
Moscow

To a Cold Beauty

I admit—you are amazing,
like a drop of dew on a petal.
I admit—you are a temple for every eye,
like a drop of dew on a petal.
Yet, I am bored with your nonchalance
as I am with my expired passport.
I am mountainous.
The slightest touch
boils my blood like flame,
and you are cold,
like a drop of dew on a petal.

4.6.1975
Moscow

Dream

I can't sleep:
I'm afraid if I leave, I'll lose you.
I can't sleep:
our remaining days
can be counted on fingers.
They are drops of dew under the sun.
I'm afraid if I leave, I'll lose you.
I can't sleep.

Sleep, my love.
Think of a sea
as still as your eyes.
Think of a sky
as silent as my agony.
Don't let sadness consume you, be still, rest.
Yesterday I had a pleasant dream:
human beings had thousands of hands.
Each hand
like a tree
branches into thousands of fingers.

11.7.1975
Egumenko

Prophecy

I am not a fortune teller—
I do not read horoscopes
or the lines of fate on a palm.
Still I know, it is clear to me,
that as long as you love me
you will be a soft song
for gypsies to sing
on winter nights.
You will become a line
written by the sun at dawn,
buried by the murderers of verse at sunset.

1.11.1975
Moscow

If Once More I Return

I

If once more I return,
in the morning,
every morning,
I will roll in the clover pastures
like a newborn lamb.
I will savor a blade of bitter grass
and run my feet through the cold dew
until I fall, exhausted.

If once more I return,
I will climb the heights of the walnut trees
like a squirrel.
A wisp of low cloud,
I will ramble over green meadows.
Like a weeping willow
I will bow over rivers
    and the shore's rocks.
Oh, to return.

If once more I return,
I will observe
how the ears of wheat yellow,
how the apples and pomegranates ripen,
how the pin-tailed sand grouse
weaves its nest.

I will observe
how its young learn their wings,
how the migrant swallows
land on the roadside electrical wires,
    how they make their lines,

where the rivers come from
and where they go.

If once more I return,
I will sip
from each spring's breast:
they are all mothers of mine.
I will lay my head
on a stone in a different cave each night:
they are all cradles of mine.

If once more I return,
I will bring tongues of fire
to those without tongue.
I will bring wings of fire
to those without wings.

If once more I return,
I won't allow the young
to pick up flowers
to display in dead vases.
I will teach them: when they go
to their lovers, before they embrace,
pin flowers on the lapel.

The blue-eyed children of Moscow have taught me
never to enter a home without sweets.
If once more I return,
I will make many soft, simple swings for children.
On the day of their birth,
though they don't know what a birthday is,
I will celebrate.
Instead of candles,
I will light my fingers,
I will light the pupils of my eyes,
I will light my newest verses.

If once more I return,
I will gently bow over any cradle
I come across.
Ah, children, if only I can return.

II

Mother,
I remember
when I was a child
I so loved the bitter taste of earth
that I chewed on the clay.
You struck me
and made me spit it out.

Mother,
I am no longer that child,
and if I return to Berkot,
even if you curse
the milk you gave me,
I will weave with my childhood needles.
Trees, stones, earth, clay,
whatever I meet: I will take into my mouth.

17.12.1975
Moscow

Exile

When exile blows like a storm
over the plains of my peace,
when sadness like the black crow
at the threshold of my room
opens its wings and hovers,
I take the frozen-winged sparrow
of my grief and
I go, I go
to find a child
who with his sunny eyes can thaw
the wings of my sparrow and remind it how to fly.
But, my dear,
with my own eyes, many times I have seen
that when the children
in this city grieve,
they waddle like little ducks
to bathe in the lake of your eyes.

27.12.1975
Moscow

Last Winter

When you were with me last winter
in our city
even the ice
bloomed with sweet william.
Even icicles
as they hung from trees and eaves turned green.

When you were with me last winter
the rain didn't drench me,
the gales couldn't freeze my fingers.

When you were with me last winter
the rush of the Sirwan River
    was with me,
an ear of wheat from Garmyan, [3]
a snowflake of Kohestan [4]
    was with me.

1975
Moscow

---

[3] The warm plains from Hawler (Erbil) to Kirkuk
[4] The cool mountainous region Kurds retreat to with their flocks in summer

Oh, Far-off Mountain Peoples

Oh, far-off mountain peoples,
I no longer believe
in border lines,
the distance between two places,
the alphabet of geography,
the colorful maps.

You have caught me
the way fire catches a man.

The faster I run,
the farther I go,
I see you rise higher,
greater, nearer.

The morning finds not one house
I haven't visited.
The evening finds not one corner
I haven't made safe for lovers.

When one of your babies cries
I will comfort him.
The sick insomniac,
I will give him heart.

You celebrate, dancing—
I catch the lead.
You mourn at the funeral—
I die before the dead.

Oh, far-off mountain peoples,
I no longer believe
in border lines,

the distance between two places,
the alphabet of geography,
the colorful maps.

11.6.1976
Berlin

Waiting

I am waiting for you.
You will come back, I swear.
I swear, you will come back.

If one by one they mine the borders,
if they riddle the world with bullets,
every day
with the dawn
I will unspool my glance toward the skyline.
I feel
you will enter the skin
of a mythical bird
and come back to me one morning.

You will come back, I swear.
I swear, you will come back.
If they guard the skies
span by span,
every day
with the dawn
I will open my windows.
I feel
you will become a vine
sprouting
one morning
below my window,
climbing the wall
        to come back to me.

21.6.1976
Moscow

Three Poems

I

I promise you nothing.
I know, now,
how much I love you.
Now, like hemoglobin
you move in my blood.

My heart is not a box
that will hold you, unchanging, until my death.
You are not fruit
and my heart is no factory
to can and preserve you.
I promise you nothing.
I know, now,
how much I love you.
Now, like hemoglobin
you move in my blood.

7.10.1976
Moscow

II

When I put my head on your downy thigh,
oh, sweet girl,
I am more tranquil
than a dove that
circles the feet of Pushkin's statue.
When your downy thigh falls asleep,
and I bear the weight my own head,

I will be lonelier than
the poem whose essence
has been martyred.

14.7.1976
Egumenko

III

I am a riddling tangle.
I am a mythical cave.
I am a lantern:
for an instant, for you, I ignite.
Night and day, I burn out.

I am dense like
the jungle of your country.
I am teeming like
the jungle of your country.
No question's footsteps can find a path to me.

If you want
to undress me like a dagger,
if you want
my mysteries, like wild fish,
to surface at your glance,
if you want
to crack my chest open,
wide as the sea,
take me under an oak tree,
take me to a mountain's peak.

15.7.1976
Egumenko

Vigilance

The night is half-gone.
Sleep, my darling,
put your head on my palm or take my shoulder.
Don't wait for me tonight—
I will guard you, I won't sleep.

You are a light sleeper.
Nature scowls and pants.
I'm afraid that
every gust of wind,
every rustling tree,
every roar in the clouds
or the rushing rain
will, God forbid, wake you
and sever the fine links of your dream's chain.

Sleep, my darling,
put your head on my palm or take my shoulder.
Don't wait for me tonight—
I will guard you, I won't sleep.

8.12.1976
Berlin

You Will Leave Me, Too

written for a song

You will leave me, too.
How well I know: you will leave me.
You will get drunk and,
empty as the bottle, you will leave me.

You will leave me, too,
the way grass leaves the summer garden,
the way fog leaves the mountains,
you will leave me, too.

You will leave me, too,
the way a mustang throws her rider,
the way feverish words leave the lips,
you will leave me, too.

If you know that this time
you have made your final decision,
change your address,
erase our footprints
from under this city's sky.
Then, God be with you.
The way a mustang throws her rider:
leave me that way.
The way feverish words leave the lips:
leave me that way.

28.10.1976
Moscow

Comfort

Don't worry if I have written
poems for other beauties.
In their faces
I saw only yours.

My heart is dark as a tunnel,
light the remains of a candle.
Come, press your cheek on my chest
the way Kurds clasp their mountains.
I want
to assure your eyes,
green as the terebinth's first fruit,
I swear to you,
in you, I see no one else.

29.11.1976
Moscow

Before the Thunder

We can
delay winter
or, when it comes,
steal its hurricane,
ice, and snow.

We can
give the sky's serenity
to the furious sea,
the sea's bottomlessness to the sky.

If you have decided
to destroy a temple,
I won't beg you not to.
I will bring you a pickaxe.
If you have decided
to destroy the nest,
I won't beg you not to.
I will bring a stone to fill your hand.
But before you
sharpen the pickaxe,
before you stone the feathered nest,
let me tell you,
before it's too late,
we can
delay winter
or, when it comes,
steal its hurricane,
ice, and snow.

11.12.1976
Moscow

A Message

It's evening.
The rain slowly, slowly falls.
I am lonely.
No, I am not.
All Moscow shares my steps.
My loneliness was a fawn
that a hunter startled with a shot:
it outpaces me.

It's evening.
The rain slowly, slowly falls.
I am lonely.
No, I am not.
I walk,
the crowded streets tangle around my legs.
I walk,
in my pocket
a message in a scarlet envelope
beats like my second heart.

1.5.1977
Moscow

Your Eyes

If in a dense forest I stray,
if in a restless ocean
a whirlpool rages around my boat,
I won't be afraid
as long as your eyes compass and guide me,
as long as your eyes give me close harbor.

Let others give their ears to the radio
for the forecast.
I, when evening comes,
I give my eyes to yours.
Then I know where the wind will come from,
the temperature, and its range,
which pastures the rain will water,
which forest, which mountains it will wash.

16.8.1977
Potsdam

Beate

The train, like a pursued snake,
slithered and hissed
The night had the scent of lovers' meetings,
autumn,
poetry,
rain.

She said, *My name is Beate.*
I kept silent.
She kept silent. She drew out a cigarette.
I lit it for her.
Little by little,
the cigarette between her fingers
became ash
and I, who had been ashes before,
little by little,
became a blazing cigarette
between her lips.

She dozed off.
A hand with violet nail polish
like a sealed message
of coup d'etat
crept into my hand and settled.
Her head, a poem, slowly, slowly
inclined onto my shoulder, which,
like a notebook,
was eager
for a new poem.

All night she slept.
All that cold night, like a merchant
just home from a journey,
I counted the gold and silver of her dreams.

In the morning,
when the train's seizures had ceased,
I found my head on Prague's knee.
The sleeping queen, Beate,
woke up.
Guten morgen!
Guten morgen!
She took her bag, left the train,
didn't gave me her address,
didn't say good-bye.

Ah! Beate,
if only I knew
on whose shoulder your head rested
that night,
who was the knight
who rode through your dreams?
Ah! Beate,
if only I knew.

22.8.1977
Prague

Kurdistan

Fields sing for rain, mountains for eagles,
rivers for running, sun for horizons,
magi for hearths, wind for leaves,
moons and stars for daylight, and I for you,
my Kurdistan, I for you.

5.10.1977
Moscow

I Am Two People

I am two people—
we sway like two moon beams,
my arms your waistband,
at the same time
among the mountain's children,
in a ring of fire,
I line up to *shayi*.[5]

I am two people:
when you look at my lips
you see a smile.
When you look at my eyes
you see the hint of tears.
I am two people.

4.12.1977
Moscow

---

[5] Shayi, also known as halparke, is a form of Kurdish dancing. Participants hold hands or link elbows to form lines and dance in various formations: short or long lines, rings, concentric circles, lopsided geometries forced by the shape of a space.

The Talisman

My land is an incantation
thousands of years old,
given to me by Noah
given to me by Noah who warned me,
Take care, don't let anyone speak it.
If spoken it will lose all power.

7.8.1978
Kreifswald

A Slap in the Face

Do you want the sun?
It is there, deep in the horizon.
Take up your daggers, stab the sky, drag the sun out!

Do you want to find your lost face?
A caliph made clay from it
for the bricks of the first mosque.
Go! Destroy the mosques.

What do you want?
Your independence?
Your independence
is a girl who has slept beside you for a thousand years.
But where, where is your manhood?

8.8.1978
Neubrandenburg

The Unknown Soldier

When a delegate visits a foreign country
he brings a crown of flowers
for the grave of the unknown soldier.

If tomorrow
a delegate came to my country
and asked me,
Where is the grave of the unknown soldier?

I would say:
Sir,
at the bank of each stream,
under the cupola of each mosque,
at the threshold of each house, each church, each cave,
under every mountain's boulders,
under every garden's branches.
In this country,
over any fist of earth,
under any shred of sky,
don't be afraid, bow your head
and set down your crown of flowers.

5.11.1978
Moscow

Come Clean

From sunrise to sunset, the sun wanders the sky,
but he never forgets his horizon.
A river winds in thousands of directions,
but still it flows to the sea.

Between our meeting
and departure, lover,
there are many embraces,
but all
show me the path to yours.

2.1.1979
Moscow

Harmony

Without you
I am a grain of sand
roaming the vast orbit of the universe.
With you
the orbit of the universe constricts:
it becomes a ring,
that fits any of my words' fingers.

10.3.1979
Moscow

I Love You and Her As Well

I live only once.
Either I love you or her.
I live only once.
Either I will grieve the light of day
or the sheen of night.

If I lived twice
you would be my only love in this life,
she my only in the second.
But what can be done?
I live only once.
I have no choice.
I must love you and her as well.
I must worship both the light of day
and the sheen of night as well.

16.3.1979
Moscow

Union

I don't know how to become one with you.
If you're heaven, then tell me.
I will kneel to every god.
If you're hell, then tell me.
I will fill the Earth with sin.

I don't know how to become one with you.
If you're an occupied territory, tell me.
I will make my skin your flag.
If you are, as I am, a gypsy,
draw a border around me:
make me your country.

Moscow
2.4.1979

Resurrection

From time to time, sadness fills my throat
and pain reaches its limit.
Then, I wish to smash my life
like a wine glass against stone.
But suddenly
the gleam of the thread of a new idea,
imagination's hide and seek,
the revival of a blade of grass,
the burst of an infant's laughter,
the figure of beauty,
the rebellious breasts of an ample woman
compel me
to take wings from happiness,
to beg the heavens
to stretch the bridge of my life so long
I won't be able to cross it, even in a thousand years.

9.5.1979
Moscow

Condition

No, I am not against dictators.
Let them rule throughout the world
like the shadow of God,
but on one condition:
let children be the dictators.

22.10.1979
Berlin and Warsaw

Title

Until I finish a poem
I scratch at my soul
        as if I were carding cotton.
When it's done,
I give it a period as a throne
then crown it with a title.

If a swan
even once rinsed its wings
        in the sea of my passion,
it becomes a word for the poem
that I write endlessly.

My friend, I am tired.
My poem continues to grow,
yet the poems of existence have
already been collected in full.
I'm aware:
in my memory,
words begin to change places.
Let me place the period
and make you the title.

19.11.1979
Moscow

Confusion

On the day we will see each other,
whatever I reach my hand toward,
teacups, books, pens:
all leak fragrance.

On the day we will see each other,
it's early, you're still far,
but my body parts compete:
my eyes pick fruit from the orchard of your body,
my hands climb your voice,
my ears sink in your scent
    and measure the distance between us.
I wish you could know
how scatterbrained I become
    the day we will see each other.

22.11.1979
Moscow

The Unbidden Prayers of Exile

I

Wherever I see a mountain
my heart,
as at my lover's first touch,
beats,
throbs.
I stand at its base, amazed:
I see
all the world's mountain chains
descend from the mountains of my homeland.

II

Wherever I see a spring
my heart,
as at my lover's first touch,
beats,
throbs.
Before I sip its water,
I sink to my knees, serene:
I comb its green moss
as if it were my beloved's hair.
I see
all the world's sweet water
springs from the headwaters of my homeland.

III

I have seen the cold of strange cities,
but my fingers never froze,
for the cold world conceals
a ray of sun from my homeland.

I have seen the heat of strange cities,
but my spirit never flagged,
for every heat conceals
a cool breeze from my homeland.

IV

The eyes of European girls,
whether blue or green,
enchant me:
in the bluest eye,
    in the greenest,
        in this world,
a tinge of black, the black
    of the eyes of women
    from my homeland.

V

My homeland,
you are a film over my eyes.
You surround me.
You are a mirror in which
I see the whole world reflected.
You are a hedge:
because of you I see nothing—
no horizon, no earth,
no God, no sky.
I don't know if
the world is as small as you are
or if you are as big as the world,
my homeland, Kurdistan.

29.11.1979
Moscow

Charred Forest

Every time a woman gave me her heart,
I planted it as a sapling
    in these foothills of mine.
Under the shade
of my lovers,
I ranged a wondrous forest.

When I met you,
willowy, immortal sapling,
I thought you would join the others,
be planted, and grow to give
a breeze in summer,
warmth in winter,
but all of a sudden you became a matchstick
who set fire to my lands.

30.11.1979
Moscow

The Free World

The free world has listened for so long
to the pulse of oil deep in the earth
that it has grown deaf and hunchbacked.
Mountain peaks can fall under fire
and the free world doesn't hear or see.

1979
Moscow

Tonight, Until the Sun Rises

All night, I couldn't sleep. I gazed at you.
Several times you shuddered.
Several times you cried out.
What were you dreaming of?
Why did you shudder?
Was it the neighing of sorrow's horse?
The sparks from my pen?
The igniting and extinguishing of my fire?
The ceaseless soaring and perching?

What was it, dear?
In your dreams, did you see me with another woman?
Was I packing to return home?

I am not afraid of your sorrows.
I know
your sorrows
compared to other sorrows
are bits of glass beads and pearls:
small, endearing, adorable.

So, my dear,
once more fill my soul
with childhood and the desire to play.
Empty your pockets–
scatter
your beads and pearls.

Winter, 1979
Moscow

Insanity

I know you are only a word,
but many times I have sacrificed a poem
      for the sake of a single word.

I know you are only a bud,
but many times I have ignored a whole garden
to cherish a single bud.

11. 1979
Moscow

Idea

These days,
like a swift, white bird,
the idea of a new poem
harries me.
However I hide myself,
it tears through the clouds of my thought,
then fades.

I am restless.
Who knows
when this wild bird will perch?
When will I tame it?
When will it grow accustomed to me?
Just like a woman:
run after her and she eludes me.
Retreat and she follows me.

29.1.1980
Budapest

The Red Notebook

The satisfied countries of the world
have a red notebook
for those birds and animals
whose killing is forbidden.

I beg UNESCO,
in its red notebook
record my name as well.
Save my skin and fur
from hunters and merchants.

What can I do?
I'm not reptilian: I can't slither
into the gorge at a rustling,
crossing ditch and ridge like a wind.
Neither am I a brute
who can grab his cub with his canines
and make a cave his den.

What can I do?
I am not a bird: evicted from earth
I can't open the door of the sky with my wings.
Neither am I a fish: when the whirlpool rises,
I can't descend into the ocean's depths for shelter,
where not even imagination's eyes can discover me.

I exist and don't on these two feet
and drones, on their two feet, sting me,
swarm me,
right and left, up and down.
Head to toe, I am all wounds.
Shelter me,
give me refuge, red notebook.

2.6.1980
Moscow

Silence

When I am silent, don't talk to me.
Don't shake the twig of my tongue
until the fruit is ripe.

I am not the only one who is silent.
Look:
    how mute
the boulders are
as they expose their chests to thunder.
Look:
    how mute
the grass is
as it stretches its blades toward the light.

When I am silent,
don't think that I'm unburdened or idle.
Trust me:
my cranium is a beehive, hectic.

I have told you so much about my homeland.
Your soul is brimming with love for it.
You hope to go
and brighten your eyes with its cities and villages.
Do you want to touch its wounds?
Then, when I am silent,
saddle my silence,
put your feet in the stirrups and strike:
you will see my whole homeland.

5.8.1980
Potsdam

Suicide

I feed my verses with my own blood
even though I know they deplete my soul.
In its folds, the night carries sunbeams
even though it is aware
that the sun's first spear will pierce its liver.

18.8.1980
Potsdam

Habit

Every day at dawn,
I soak my heart
in the rays of the sun,
in red electric current.
As a letter, I envelope it and give it to the wind
who freely chooses,
and I never ask who will receive it.

18.8.1980
Moscow

How I Dread

I dread
that when I return
you will have bitter news.

I dread
embracing you
and smelling a stranger.

I dread
that when I return
the grammar of your eyes,
the alphabet of your gestures will have changed.

I dread
that the temperature of your fingers
will have risen or fallen.

And, more so,
how I dread, my friend,
that when I return
not you, but I will have changed.

28.10.1980
Vienna

Separation

Every night,
when a pillow
invites our two heads
like the poles of the Earth
to the table of sorrow,
separation
lays like a dagger,
shining between us.
Staring at it,
I can't sleep.
I wonder if you see the same.

Every night, when a pillow
invites our two heads
like the poles of the Earth
to the table of sorrow,
my heart shrinks like
a ball before death's mallet.
I am terrified to die before you,
but I will lose my mind if you die before me.

7.12.1980
Moscow

Snowstorm

A snowstorm at dusk:
I made a nest from my palm
for a snowflake, adrift.
I gazed at it until it melted.
As a drop of water, I recognized it
from a spring in Kurdistan!

12.1.1981
Moscow

Contemplation

My friend,
yesterday evening
I yearned for you.
I brooded,
contemplating the horizon.
Can you imagine what the sun looked like?
A fair-haired girl, beheaded.
Right then, I resolved
I would burn my tongue
if I ever compared you again to the sun.

18.2.1981
Potsdam

Meeting

Friend,
tell me,
who betrayed our secret meeting?
Whose hand shakes
the clove pinks in this dark midnight?

From the moment you arrived,
moonlight has stolen in,
breezes flirt with the curtains,
leaves lean to leaves
to gossip.

Friend,
tell me,
who betrayed our secret meeting?
Whose hand shakes
the clove pinks in this dark midnight?

16.7.1981
Potsdam

A River

Though you and I have coalesced
like the soil of one land,
what can I do?
My homeland, a river,
constantly
overruns and divides us:
its riverbanks.

17.7.1981
Moscow

Fear

The higher the snow,
the more it fears the sun.
The prettier the woman,
the brighter the lamp of aging
burns in her sight.
In this world
each bears some fear.
Owl: the populous.
Thief: the dog's bark,
the insomniac's cough.
Donkey: the steep ascent.
Wall: the spike.
Wood: the nail.
Ibex: the clatter of shifting stone,
the whispering of leaves.
I, too, fear
that at my dying moment my lungs will scream
for just a sip of my mother country's air.
I fear they will bury me in soil
that doesn't understand my tongue,
that bears a foreign scent.

15.1.1982
Potsdam

For a Gypsy

I

Stop staring into my palm.
I don't want you to tell me
how many children I will father,
whether I will become rich or remain broke.
Tell me one thing only:
will I remain as you are until I die
or will I gain a country of my own?

25.2.1980
Moscow

II

Your sky extends the length of your footstep.
Keep your head bowed.
Keep your neck humble.
Don't look
for the stars, the sky, or God.
For one without a measure of land,
where is God? The stars? The sky?

18.1.1982
Potsdam

III

Don't worry.
Don't trouble yourself. I say this for your sake:
no one can read my palm.
Only I know the secret—
it's not a palm.
It's a map of valleys, mountains, and streams.

29.2.1982
Moscow

Masterpiece

My poems are diverse:
some are cities,
others villages,
some palaces,
others huts,
but the one I dedicate to you
is my masterpiece:
the brightest capital in the world.

6.1982
London

For Hundreds of Years

For hundreds of years,
my own house in ruins,
I have served like a blind cat in the corners of the Sultan's
kitchen.
For hundreds of years,
my own gate unguarded,
I have stood sentry at the thieves' door.

For hundreds of years,
one day, I am
a stable boy for the Governor of Baghdad,
another, textiles in Tehran,
another, sackcloth
to scour the Sultana's hips,
and yet another, a broom to sweep Damascus clean.

For hundreds of years,
like a handful of grain,
the mill of history ground me down.
Anthills appeared all around me,
ants swarmed over me.

For hundreds of years,
my cranium has been a minaret:
open to any loud mouth.
For hundreds of years,
my homeland has been a narghile
for anyone to put between their teeth and pull at.

For hundreds of years,
I have been a pair of patched sandals
before the world's gate.
I have fit any foot.

For hundreds of years,
torn, they threw me away.
For hundreds of years,
patched, they wore me yet again.

I am a wounded back:
I rose against the whip.
I am a reckless flood:
I rise against shores
that have become confining.
I don't pool,
I don't rest.
I am on edge.
My tranquility was a light:
a hurricane snuffed it out.
I am no longer mercy.
My mercy was an ocean.
They put their mouths to it and they drank it down.
I don't pool,
I don't rest.
When I am a single grain, what chance do I have?
       It's me or the ant.
When I am a drop of blood, what chance do I have?
       It's me or the leech.

Only a whore would say
the grain and the ant are brothers.
Only a whore would say
blood and the leech are brothers,
the fish and the spear,
the mouse and the feed sack,
the hand and the stinger are brothers.
The whores say
the rope and the neck,
the razor and the hair are brothers.

Come, people,
ask pain, ask prey,
ask, for God's sake,
does there exist a dagger that heals the wound?
Is there a hunter who doesn't devour his prey?

Oh, people, ask hay,
has it seen a cold fire?
Ask the bird,
has a snake ever jutted his jaw into the nest
intending to kiss?

Come on, ask oak,
has it seen an axe that doesn't cut wood?
Come on, ask the donkey,
has it seen a wolf that won't tear him apart?

The whores say
there is a snake with sweet poison.
The whores say
there is an axe who is brother to the woods.

I am a wounded back:
I rose against the whip.
I am a reckless flood:
I rise against shores
that have become confining.
I don't pool,
I don't rest.
I am on edge.
My tranquility was a light:
a hurricane snuffed it out.
My mercy was an ocean.
They put their mouths to it and they drank it down.

2.9.1982
Potsdam and Berlin

Happiness

Earthly happiness is like the sun,
sometimes visible, other times imperceptible.
I yearn to soar through the heavens,
a thief,
to capture you
a happiness that never withers,
that no misery can approach.
Such happiness from the heavens
in the sky—only the stars possess—
on Earth—no one but you.

25.9.1982
Moscow

Illusion

Tonight I'm drunk,
    distracted,
       dull.
On the throne of my unruly brain
a woman I don't know sits, crowned.

7.4.1983
Moscow

Sleeplessness

This night, like all those past,
my sleep, a skittish fawn,
has abandoned its den: my eyes.
Your happiness is a treasure.
Afraid it will be stolen
I sit up beside it, watchful.

11.12.1983
Moscow

If an Apple...

If I have an apple, I will split it:
half for you, half for me.

If I am given a smile, I will split it:
half for you, half for me.

If I stumble on grief, I will keep it to myself
and devour it alone, as if it were my last breath.

31.12.1983
Prague

Treasure

Since the world began,
men have made lovers of jewelry, gold, and silver.
For them they have searched the seas
                        and mountain peaks.
But every morning
I find treasure:
your hair, undone,
flowing over half my pillow.

10.8.1984
Odessa

Chandelier and Candle

There are those who need
a glorious chandelier
to find their way to the S[2]ultan's heart.

There are those who need
only the remains of a candle
to see and set fire to their inner self.

Whenever I reach
for the pen,
I check
what is burning.
The chandelier or the candle?

12.8.1984
Moscow

Woman

I

Looking at you,
I return to the Stone Age,
to dark caves and thick jungles.
I listen reverently
to lightning, roaring clouds, rushing rain.
This civilization of buttons and wires grows faint.
The sacred fires blaze again.

II

Whatever you want will be done.
With a glance,
you can make green lands barren.
With a gesture,
you can turn lands of stone to meadow.

Whatever you want will be done.
You can
bind the wings of my tongue.
    You can forbid the tree of my fingers fruit.
Fill the stream of my voice with fish—
it is in your hands.
    You can transform each word of mine into a pearl.
You can
reduce me to a slave under the yoke
Crown me in glory—
it is in your hands.

III

Under a heap of ash—
you are a glowing ember of fervent hope.

In the whorl of darkness—
you are glittering mountain snow.

In the desert—you are a roaring creek,
in famine—steaming bread
in strange lands—a shelter.
You possess the keys to paradise.
You are not half, but the whole world.

28.11.1985
Tripoli

Congress of Bottles

Yesterday, there was a congress,
a congress of bottles.
Each country sent a representative
who
briefly recounted what he had been through:
how many coffee shops and houses he had searched,
how many tables he had crowned,
how many mouths he had touched and what had filled him.

Before the congress concluded,
a black bottle,
brooding and scowling and silent since morning,
rose and came to the microphone:
"Sisters and brothers,
like you, I have been used,
but I have seen no tables, no lovers' meetings,
no village journeys, no city bars.
Do you want the truth?
I have come all this way
so I can tell you
I have seen nothing but people
who the Ba'athists shoved me into
front and back.

Tripoli
30.1.1986

You Grieve

You grieve
for widows,
for widowers,
for orphans.
I grieve, too, but more
for those fairies and knights
who now can never be born.

16.11.1986
Tripoli

Birth

I hear the cries of my nation.
I trust
tomorrow's world will be bright
for I have seen childbirth:
it begins with
kicking and screaming.

20.5.1987
Tripoli

Museum

In tomorrow's Kurdistan,
I will build the world's biggest museum,
with an enormous exhibit for each period.
The first I will name
The Prehistoric Age.
The remaining exhibits:
Claws, Fangs, and *Bayonets.*

1.11.1988
Tripoli

Hope

While
above, on mountain peaks,
blizzards rage at shrubs and trees,
don't worry—
below, in the valleys,
tender sprouts spring up.

25.12.1988
Tripoli

Sunflower

My homeland—
    is the nest of the sun,
       a bright rayfield.
My head is not a head,
but an ever-inclined sunflower.

13.4.1989
Tripoli

Halabja

I

I won't be shocked if here and there
I see that some humans,
instead of teeth, have fangs,
instead of nails, claws.
What shocks me, like a miracle of God,
is that the one who strangled Halabja
had two eyes and walked on two legs.

14.4.1989
Tripoli

II

Thousands of
screams and sobs stuck in the throat.
Thousands of questions
flew to God's kingdom.
They all fell, strangled on their way.
And now, day and night,
I am in misery.
Nothing soothes me,
whether awake or in bed,
I want ask who I should damn:
Satan or the One Who Whistled?[6]

14.4.1989
Moscow

---

[6] In Kurdish folklore, a whistle will call Satan. The poet's mother, when he would whistle as a boy, would always say, "Hush! Do you want to bring the devil here?"

During the Bombardment

Fire rains down.
Which to carry?
Which to rescue?

The eldest is sick,
the other is toddling,
eyes all pupil and a mouth full of tongue.

I had two hands.
The enemy took one of them.
The other remains.

Which to carry?
Which to rescue?
One is my heart's thread,
the other the pupil of my eye.

1990
Tripoli

Here and There

Every night
I lay on my back
and listen to the silence speak:
Be patient.
At dawn, when the sun reaches you,
it will harness a chestnut horse
and give you bread for the trip.

Then, until the sun rises,
here, my body is stump,
there, my spirit stampedes.

When the sun
cracks the eggshell of the horizon
    and chokes the neck of my lamp,
its first rays
    come to me like the postman:
Where are you going,
you rapid pain?
Don't you know
executioners at the borders
have closed the roads?
Your homeland is a tangle of arrows and knives.
Don't hurry.
Wait for darkness:
darkness is the citadel of men.[7]

It has been eighteen years—
eighteen springs,
eighteen summers,
eighteen falls,

[7] Common Kurdish proverb.

eighteen winters,
eighteen ages without Kurdistan—
night gives me up to the first rays of the sun.
They say:
Why hurry?
Wait till night.
It has been eighteen years.
I myself am lost:
I don't know if
I'm here or there.

16.7.1991
Minsk

The Dagger

I am a naked dagger,
my motherland a stolen sheath.
Don't think me bloodthirsty.
Incriminate instead
the one who unsheathed me.

16.7.1991
Minsk

On the Funeral of a Poem

My head was an ocean.
Thoughts, like baitfish,
sank and surfaced.
I threw my net all night.
I caught only one fish:
flipping and flopping on shore, it died.

1991
Moscow

The Little Hand from Chamchamal

It was 1992.
I was in Chamchamal.
For spring, it was late,
for summer, early.
The trenches of the enemy,[8] close
as the bullet can fly, were coiled.
A child took his hand, the color of a lemon,
from the hand of his mother, dressed in black.
He came to me, took my hand, and made it his own.

Since that day,
tightly, so tightly, he has held my hand.
I beg
him to release me, even for a second,
but my pleas are taken with the wind.

Whatever is said,
whatever is written
about my freedom and audacity,
it is all a lie,
it is all mythology.
The time has come to confess:
my pen is also enslaved,
neither boundless nor free.
What commands it is that slight hand,
the color of a lemon.

10.5.1992
Hawler

---

[8] The Ba'athists

Meditation

It was the beginning.
Crimson set fire to the hem of the sky
and filled my body's cells
with hissing flame.
It sent its eldest ray with bread for my voyage.
It pointed
to a crooked path.

Now,
dusk has fallen, I am tired of the road.
The pale rays of the sunset
caress my forehead.
The footfall of stars reach my ear.
I am sunk in sweat and dusk.
Only one hill remains before me.
On the other side, a heavy fog
holds a small resting place.
One uphill, one ascent,
one downhill, one descent.
But how can I go?
I have no dawn bread left,
no more hissing flame within me,
and the earth clutches my ankles,
begging for a gift.
Oh, God, what do I have, what to leave the earth?

13.7.1992
Moscow

Martyr

Last night, my sleep was fitful.
I crept outside,
my mind throwing thunder.
Lifting my head to the sky,
I saw naked stars,
clusters and clusters, thousands and thousands.
Around the roosting swan,
they were scattered like pomegranate seeds.
I went back inside
and mourned for them,
for those stars
with wounded wings and broken necks
who, at the height of their brilliance,
plummet from the heavens head first.

13.7.1992
Moscow

Raving

A cottage at the mountain's foot,
the drip, drip of a drizzling rain,
a fireplace,
the crackling of twigs and branches,
a shelf full of books,
a bright, sweet-cheeked, baby,
a dusky beloved,
curls and wisps falling to her waist and
earrings in her ears,
a thin sorrow, hiding and seeking,
a murmur, a murmur, a far stream through the forest,
a kettle of brewing tea over a dense fire,
a bowl of buttermilk from the cellar,
two or three hot loaves of bread,
a basket full of pomegranates and
sweet-smelling black grapes.

19.7.1992
Shukina

Age

As long as you are with me, dearest,
what do I need from the months or years?
Even as a newborn,
my heartache's beard was white.
    I thought happiness impossible,
but now, thanks to your love,
even under the heavy burden of years,
I am taking my first steps, my mouth full and stumbling.

12.6.1993
Cherikovo

Comparison

It was midnight.
Nature was still, the world insensate.
You slept,
your cheek on the back of your hand.
I observed you.
A breeze of wallflowers lifted me up.
An eternal melody unsettled me.
I closed the book in my hands,
freed myself from its confinement,
and began to read your sacred face,
gently, gently, verse by verse,[9] until day broke.

13.6.1993
Cherikovo

---

[9] The word for "verse" used here, ayat, is not for poems, but for verses of the Qu'ran.

A Draft

I am a draft.
Time writes me, sketches me
like a craftsman until
the day when
I will be printed—by the coffin,
bound—by the grave,
and published—at my wake.

4.7.1993
Moscow

You Think

You think
my poems
are simple as roadside stones?
You think
my words
are not astronauts, but earthbound children?
What can I do, my heart?
Images and thin ideas
shimmer for a moment
and die like fireflies
    in the black nights of gardens and orchards.
I can only catch those
that tire and fall
    like autumn leaves.

14.7.1993
Moscow

Good Morning

Good morning
to you girls of the next century.
Good morning
to you boys of the next century.
Keep your eyes on the road:
don't think I am far away.
That promise I made you?
Even now, I insist on it.
Keep your eyes on the road:
I must meet you, it must be.
Don't ask when,
don't ask how,
don't doubt: I will return.
Maybe
on Nawroz Day,
on Mala Marwan Hill,
like grass from a dry root,
I will spring up.
Perhaps one night
with a bolt of lightning
I will strike.
For a while, like a ghostly flag,
I will flap before all eyes.
Maybe
just after a heavy rain,
I will rise as a mushroom
at the foot of a birch tree
Or as an ear of flowering barley
on the plains of Qaraj.
Or in the heat of dancing
I will press myself into the crowd and
suddenly come to a girl's hands.

Good morning
to you girls of the next century.
Good morning,
to you boys of the next century.
When you see me,
call me
to your full table.
I am sure
your bread doesn't taste of blood and fear.
Let me sleep one calm night
in your bed.
In this life I have searched the world so.
My bed was
either a raft on the waves
or a tree branch in a black wind's mouth.

Just once, let me,
in the middle of the road, in broad daylight,
without the mullah's judgment or tribe's permission,
released from fear, careless of blame,
fully intertwine with a Kurdish girl
whose breath smells of daffodils,
whose palms taste of the earth.

Good morning
to you girls of the next century.
Good morning,
to you boys of the next century.
I yearn
for that day:
the day of return, of striking,
the day of flowering and rising.
Prepare a passport for me.
It's not important:
let it be thick or thin,
rectangular or square—

It's not important.
Let it be how you wish:
yellow,
red
blue,
purple,
or black as pine tar.
My sorrow in this life:
not one day
did I carry ID stating my own origin in my pocket.
Good morning
to you girls of the next century.
Good morning,
to you boys of the next century.

14.8.1993
Chirikovo

Power

My pen is a hammer,
my words—are nails.
Wherever oppression lies,
I pierce it like heartwood.

21.8.1993
Moscow

Monologue

It is dawn:
my arm is your pillow,
my head is on the wings of the storm.

It is dawn:
I see off one flock of questions,
but another flock is on the way.

It is dawn:
one moment, a beloved friend yet alive
rests in a coffin,
    his face draped in crocus.
Another moment, a friend long dead and buried
stands before me with open eyes.

Now, when I shut my eyes,
I shut a small window
    that looked onto the past.
I pinion the hawk
    who hunts relentlessly
    in the atmosphere of the future.

I do understand
that what is past can't be captured,
that what will come is death.
I am satisfied now
with your head on my arm.

Had Eve obeyed God,
had she seen the forbidden fruit and not taken a bite,
who says you and I
would have been
you and I?
Who says the skiff of my arm
would softly rock you
on the waves of this evening?
Who says that in that paradise
there would be a little paradise like this one,
which you and I have now?

8.10.1993
Moscow

Apart

Whether it's day's end or daybreak,
bright or a rain gray,
wherever you are,
in the crevice of a cave,
    in a raucous city,
in exile
    or a cottage in your homeland,
anytime you desire,
I will rush to you as the wind does.

Do nothing, but
go, tell a tree,
    surrounded by sparrows,
go, tell a stream,
    whose little waves are awake.

13.12.1993
Moscow

Brotherkilling

(excerpts)

I

In this miserable country,
what haven't you divided
like your vineyards?
The only pride we had was our martyrs.
You have turned even them into your herd of sheep.

I don't dare carry a pen,
I don't dare wear a shirt.
Damn you,
you have divided colors.[10]

Should I say *student* or *pupil*?
Woman or *lady*?
Damn you,
you have divided even the words in the dictionary.[11]

You have divided the two shores of eternity.
Khani and Haji Qadir.[12]
You have divided earth, water, and fire.
What have you left?
Whom have you spared?
You have divided even
prostitutes, thieves and vagabonds.

---

[10] The KDP's color is yellow while the PUK's color is green. For a time, it wasn't possible to wear certain colors in certain areas without coming under threat.
[11] Both the KDP and the PUK have their own student and women's organizations. Each party systematically uses a different Kurdish word to describe these organizations. Ironically, the most neutral word for "student" in southern Kurdistan is the Arabic word, "talib."
[12] Ahmedi Khani (1651-1706) and Haji Qadiri Koyi (1817-1897) were poets and early proponents of Kurdish nationalism. Khani wrote in Kurmanji, the northern dialect, while Koyi wrote in Sorani, the southern dialect.

Like two giants, cleavers in hand,
you have cut our homeland in two.
Roaming city by city, village by village,
in each home
you have divided each hearth.

All other peoples have one history;
we have two.
All other peoples
are infected with only one leader;
we have two.

II

You Judas goats, thanks to you
Ba'athism is a restless tongue in our mouths,
Ba'athism is a ox that rapes our brains
every morning and every evening.

Who doesn't know the Ba'athists?
These thugs, butchers, and strongmen
who, just yesterday, appeared from nowhere.
Now, thanks to you, they have come back,
they have come back, but no one sees them,
as if they are ghosts of death.
They have become TNT.
They have stolen into wads of dinar.
They come with us to our table.
They share our beds.
They come with us to meet our lovers.

In the headlines of newspapers—
                    I see Ba'athism.
In the security convoys of politicians—
                    I see Ba'athism.
In parliament's split power—

I see Ba'athism.
In the killing of captives and extracting of confessions,
in midnight's ringing door bells—
I see Ba'athism.

Thanks to you,
one of my eyes dances with joy
that the other has been blinded.
One of my veins laughs hysterically
that its fraternal artery has been severed.

Thanks to you,
today, in my occupied hometown,
the Peshmerga's *jamadani*,[13]
for years a crown,
in no time, before my own eyes,
became the occupier's helmet.

III

I ring the bell,
I leave you dumb.
Full of my throat, I shout.
In the marshes,
I stir the waves to whitecap.
I disturb the dead air.

I stab thorns into your eyes.
I chase your sleep from you.
I pour salt into your wounds
to incite your pain.

---

[13] A headdress that constitutes a small woven cap held in place by a scarf that is then wound around the head.

I won't leave—
I won't leave—
I won't leave these wounds in peace—
not even your scabs and scars.
Wake up.
Don't you sleep.
We are all in one wagon
dragged behind two blind horses.

IV

Take the ribs of those martyred
during these three years of brotherkilling.
Make a full, dense jungle
right in front of them.
Let them drink tears,
take dusty blood for all three meals,
and exhale the smoke of mothers' sighs.
Put out their red eyes with thorns.
Keep
those who killed Kurds
from the next century.
God forbid, they sully that century as well.

V

My sweet, darkened city,
my dancer dressed all in black,
my occupied freedom,
my mother, my little livers,
be aware: what they give you
is poison—poison—poison.
Be aware. What they give you
is poison—thick poison.
The wine is the same,
whether this or that hand pours it.

VI

Today is not a day for poetry,
so for you I speak
in language entirely simple.
I tell you:
the Kurd who kills a Kurd
is a bastard, a pimp—cowshit.

VII

Good news: we can't die anymore.
Thanks to the headless heads,
every Kurd is now a number
in the memory of the computers
of foreign banks.

VIII

South Kurdistan, history's first born,
is an old pine tree:
hands wield a double-edged saw
and cut him down at the waist.

IX

Two corpses are thrown together, the corpses of two brothers.
Twin dreams in two different colors.

Two corpses are thrown together, the corpses of two brothers.
The distance between them is the burning sigh of their mother,
their father.
Their leaders smile.
The distance between them is
the enemy's table, the wine glass.

X

If Adam Smith and Nelson Mandela
came to my miserable country,
our leaders would hire Smith as a tea boy
in the Ministry of the Economy
and give Mandela a rifle
to guard Parliament.

5.1994
Hawler

Fall

Before the fall wind can touch me,
before I drop and burst
like the last apricot left on the branch,
I spur my imagination, a horse
like Rakhsh,[14] a conqueror of distance,
        like wind, to a gallop.

I visit the eagle's nest
and peaks under the sun.
I bar the whirlwind and the lightning from their paths.
I stand under the deluge, under the low black clouds.
I ask them all,
where will I be
when I drop dead?

Summer, 1995
Korso

---

[14] Raksh was, according to the epic Shahnameh, the horse of Rostam, the protagonist of the text. In these pre-Islamic folktales, Rostam, a hero of great physical strength, would have collapsed any horse other than Raksh, a giant among his own kind. By divine intervention, Raksh lives as long as his rider.

Peace

For a stream to entrust its secrets
                        to a neighboring stream,
for a mountain
to bend its head to another mountain,
for a tree to conquer an axe, for a whisper to conquer a roar—
I urge God—
Oh, God! Forgive me,
I do not urge You,
I only pray,
and pray ceaselessly,
make men like women
give birth to children.

17.10.1995
Korso

I Came to the World Before You

I came to the world before you
to prepare my soul
    for the feast of you,
to taste life without you,
that each moment I could
    see you would be a miracle.

I came to the world before you
to lengthen the lives of flowers
and purify the blaze of fire,
    to thin the fog of sorrow,
to learn
how to bloom over your breast,
    how to hide you fully within me.

I came to the world before you
to free fawns
from the fear
    of coming to the brook to drink,
to teach birds
to take seed from the palm,
    not from snares and traps.

I came to the world before you
so that, my dear,
whenever you desire,
    I could light the stars like candles
and make from down
a place for us to meet.

I came to the world before you
to train my eyes
to pick out your features from the typhoon of colors,
to train my ears
to find your whisper in the whirlwind of voices.

I came to the world before you
to transform each hair on my body
    into strings on which the musical score
of your body can be played,
to be worthy of holding the key
    to the throne and crown of your love.

20.10.1996
Helsinki

Since I Have Been, I Dream

Since I was, I dream.
unfading velvet dreams,
high as the stars,
fast as beam and voice.

Since I was, I sow dreams.
Day after day, year after year,
                    I sow.
From border to border, from home to home,
                    I sow.

When I write,
here and there, words rebel.
I am pedestrian—they are horsemen.
I am wingless—they are winged.
Hard as I try, I won't catch them,
far and feral as they are.
But when I fall asleep,
they make my head their hive
and poetry their honeycomb.

At times, a squirrel startles
and runs from me, branch to branch.
But when I fall asleep,
he comes to me on his own legs
and dances on my palm.

At times, the war of the stars,
Chernobyl, ruined Halabja,
Michael Jackson's mask,
the planting of men in test tubes,
the internet, and the holes in the Ozone
run after me. They unnerve me.

But when I fall asleep
the universe becomes an untouched heaven:
the stars
crack the darkness of the first night,
like quince
of the first season
they glisten on the sky's branches.

When I am awake—I see
a few drops of water
terrified under the sun.
When I fall asleep—I see
we drink sun beams,
we roar like broad rivers.

Since I was, I dream:
I am beloved—
A tan young woman from Hawler
waits for me in the airport
with a bouquet of sweet clover.
Before I can rain kisses on her
or hold her tight,
she asks,
"How was your poetry reading in Diyarbakir?"
In another dream,
I read soft poems in Mahabad,
Qamishli gives a standing ovation.

I was always so
and I remain so:
since I was, I dream.
Since I was, I sow:
in one moment,
in one hand, I take the pulse of Hamrin Peak,
in the other hand, a comb,
I untangle the waves of Wan Lake.

Another time,
one foot of mine is in Hawraman,[15]
the other
treads lightly in Afrin,[16]
until the scarf of siyachamana[17]
warms the neck of lawk.[18]

Since I was, I dream.
Since I was, I sow:
Once, just there,
in the Bayazid post office,
I saw the great Khani,
a halo of light surrounding him.
I drew closer,
amazed,
I saw we were both bewildered:
I by his greatness
and he by the express service, he could send shoes
to Balak's mountains
for Koye's[19] disciples.

Since I was, I dream.
Since I was, I sow:
at midnight
lightning hit me and I died.
My friends
in a Terebinth's shadow,
laid my corpse out
on a rose-pink slab.

---

[15] Hawraman: a Kurdish district in Iraq.
[16] Afrin: a Kurdish city in Syria.
[17] Siyachamana: a melody particular to Hawraman.
[18] Lawk: a melody particular to the Kurmanji dialect.
[19] Koye: the birthplace of the famous, nationalistic Kurdish poet, Haji Qadir Koye.

As they washed me, the water that ran off
became a stream, then a river.
Geese and cranes flew in lines.
Splashes of water and light and fog became one.
A God-given breeze rocked
the cradle of the world.
Jasmine dripped,
the sky filled with stars the color of Terebinth.
When they dressed me in my shroud,
it rose suddenly and
changed color,
became a rainbow,
soft and slim.
It didn't take long.
A soft wind blew,
I saw the many hues
ripple and become a flag.

Since I was, I dream.
unfading velvet dreams,
tall as the stars are high,
fast as beam and voice.

30.4.1997
Helsinki

Two Visitors

I host a dusky visitor.
I do not dare picture her as my motherland,
        but she is as sweet —
her voice is the shelter of an arbor
and the meadow of her breast
        smells of sweet clover.

In the corner,
an idea crouches,
undoes its braids,
and combs them, stroke after stroke,
stealthily, deliberately
cutting through the haze of my depths
        like the Gathas' beams.

Oh, God.
I don't know how
to embrace two lovers
    in the same moment?

1.8.1997
Helsinki

Reflection

The moment of reflection has come:
I have taken parcels and tattered notebooks
from the ruins of memory
and scattered them before me, a merchant.
I regret and don't
that I searched hundreds of shells
to find a single pearl of soul.

2.8.1997
Helsinki

A Footnote to the Story

The cloud who drives clouds away
and then chases after them
from league to league, from land to land:
                              It's still us.
The partridge who hunts partridges
boulder to boulder, rock to rock:
                              It's still us.

Each casket that is made for us,
plank and hammer,
spike and nail: it's still us.

Each of our cities,
their breast buttons forced open,
the thief's case man,
the thief's lookout,
and the town's night guard: it's still us.

In each garden,
the wing of a tree burns.
On each mountain
rockslides crash down. It's still us.

Each day of ours,
each month of ours,
each year of ours is hanged by
the gallows and the noose: it's still us.

If we are halved,
quartered,
cut into a thousand pieces,
the cursed scissors: it's still us.

The back and the whip, the bird and the net: it's still us.
The foot and the false step, fire and water: it's still us.

Don't let anyone spit
on those who are dead stories.
Don't let anyone point to
our absence of seas or
God's predestination or
the wrong circling of the galaxy.
No desert can catch even a mountain's feet.
We presented the desert with the mountains' peaks.

18.3.1998
Helsinki

Contractions

This midnight,
the wings of questions beat.
I am restless,
tunneling, spinning like a tornado.
Some sorrows open wide, like an ocean,
others are sealed, rolled, and stamped.

It seems to me the dough of a new poem
        has risen.
The only thing to do
is lay dry imagination down to warm the oven.

19.3.1998
Helsinki

Yearning

I am tormented,
but it's early yet.
I'll grab a few leaves,
a few blades of grass, some wild flowers.
                       from that land.
I am not afraid their names will leave my memory,
but I do fear forgetting their fragrance.

30.3.1998
Helsinki

Height

Since my beginning, I have seen
that the rose-colored road to thrones, luck, and prosperity
passes under an arch
too low for me, a crucified figure.

I have never tried to alter
my height.
Even as a sapling, storms could not make me bend.
Oh, God, help me stand tall now with my roots so deep.

28.4.1999
Helsinki

Fellow Wife

Leave me alone.
I don't need slamming doors
    or your beating footsteps.

Stay away, honey,
while I drown in verses
    dedicated to you.

29.4.1999
Helsinki

The Carnation

In a garden,
a carnation struck my fancy.
Offhanded,
I reached to pick it.
Suddenly,
I saw not the carnation on its stem,
but myself.
I trembled and thought,
I sway just like this flower,
easy, confident, calm.
Who says death's hand is not near my neck
as my hand is to this flower's?

10.6.1999
Helsinki

Enigma

For two long years,
I have been in love with a tree
growing outside my window.
No matter how many leaves clothe it,
I see it as if it were naked.
What tree? It's a woman.

Hard as I try, I don't understand:
in the spring,
when my sweet one has contractions, as she births buds,
in autumn,
when her children, those she fed from her liver, fall with the wind,
on long nights,
when the storms scream
    and she hasn't a friend in the world
but my candle burns all night,
why doesn't she come knock on my window?

10.9.1999
Helsinki

Unfinished Poem

With just words,
I have drawn a portrait of my beloved.
I consider it:
it's her exactly,
lacking only earrings for her delicate ears.

Let the dictionaries
puff their chests out,
let them grow large,
let them adorn themselves in thousands of pretty words.
What can they be worth
when they lack a word
    that I can fashion into her earrings?

I am Job,
the back of my hope will not bend,
this word obsesses me.
Sooner or later, I will reach it.
If it flies on the Simurgh's wings,
span by span I will search the sky—
if it slips underground,
among all miners, I will unearth it—
this is one word I will find
even if my imagination's
    soles blister and split.
If it cannot be found,
I will invent it.
I won't leave my love without her earrings.

20.12.1999
Gothenburg

Two Sunsets

Each evening
I gaze at the sunset.
I know,
sooner or later, I, too, will set.
But, sadly, my twilight
will not be enchanting as the sun's.

7.1.2000
Helsinki

Comfort

Don't be so upset, my sweet,
that before we met you cut your hair.

Until now, I didn't care whether
the thread of my life were to be short or long.

Now, I pray. I implore God, give me
days enough to see your hair grow out.

9.1.2000
Helsinki

The Contract

My intention:
I will dedicate a night and day of mine to you alone.
I am determined
to rein in my voyaging mind,
    to numb the waves,
to fill my home with only your murmurs.
I will shut the doors and windows and seal up every gap.

My lady,
just once,
try for yourself:
let one night and day be mine alone,
let all customs unravel,
let laws turn inside out.
Run from your surroundings,
steal yourself away from relatives and acquaintances,
from the stars and the moon,
the clouds and the blue sky,
from bickering and the little sadnesses of the world.
    Wrench yourself away.
Don't look at the hands on your watch.
Don't make yourself up, like other days.
This old world won't turn upside down.
Just this once,
for one night and one day,
kill this half-woman and become whole.
I will be yours for one night and one day.
You will be mine alone for one night and one day.

18.5.2000
Helsinki

At the Window

The sky is tattooed in stars.
The moon fills its lungs
with the blue air.
Come, throw your arms around me, watch.
Watch how
silence opens its tongue.

Come, throw your arms around me. Don't you leave me even
for a second.
I see a star
stark naked and shivering,
so young it sways.
I fear it will try to walk,
but stumble and fall.

9.12.2000
Helsinki

Hair

From time to time, your hair,
with a burst of rain, a rough wind's breath,
becomes so snarled,
so tangled,
I say, "Never—these knots will never give way."
But then, in the evenings, when it's just you and me,
in the blink of an eye, it falls free to the comb.
Again, as in the past,
it comes readily, familiar
to my palms, my breath.
It leaves the storm to storm,
the surge to surge.
I drown in waves of myrtle and sweet clover
until morning.
I admit:
whatever I know of life's philosophy,
    your hair has taught me.

6.5.2001
Helsinki

Pocket

All along
I thought I had taken care of my pockets,
patching them often,
    never leaving a single hole,
but it's hopeless—
The gash Time leaves in his pocket
lets not only moments and days, but years slip through.

29.6.2001
Helsinki

Joy

I am not used to such immense joy.
You throw a whole treasure trove under my feet
when what I most wanted was a glance.
You immerse the universe in divine light
when, for just one spark, I climbed Qaf.[20]

I am not used to such immense joy.
I beg you,
give me some time to get used to it.
I'm afraid I can't stand it,
that I will collapse under its weight.

Draw a line,
establish a border
against that insanity
which seeks the impossible and knows no limits,
establish a border against hallucination
and the fantasy of eternal youth, of stalking death,
establish a border
for those colorful birds
that rush from a thousand directions
to land on the branches of my head,
establish a border
for those meadows and grasslands
that lay naked on their backs.

I am not used to such immense joy.
It's not fair
that only for me
the night sky adorns itself with jewels of a hundred colors.

---

[20] A mythological mountain where demons live, the nest of Simurgh.

It's not fair
that only for me
the mornings
glisten with dew on the briar rose.

I am not used to such immense joy.
I beg you,
cut a bit away,
pluck a few feathers,
prune a few branches back.
For one day, two days, steal its wings.
Once, twice,
shake the branches heavy with stars.

Since the day you usurped the crown of my little kingdom,
you made me
sovereign over the universe, head to foot.
Since that day,
I have learned the language of stones,
to speak with the wind.
Since then,
I can tell colors apart by their smell,
I draw the world with water.

Since the day
you usurped my little kingdom's crown,
each stalk of grass touched by the wind,
in the mouth of the wind, I sway with it.
Since that day,
I am a galaxy without orbit
freely traversing the universe.

 am not used to such immense joy.
I beg you,
give me some time to get used to it.
I'm afraid I can't stand it—

terrified—
that I will collapse under its weight.

25.8.2003
Helsinki

Memory of a Winter's Night 1973-74

Have you ever heard of the snow
that makes the silent night blaze,
sews the night a gown from petals,
and sets the night's blood boiling with its scent?

I remember such a story:
the coldest night in the bloom of winter,
somewhere on the outskirts,
the ground their mattress, the sky their ceiling —
in the veins of two entangled bodies,
flames
transformed the midnight snow
into a meadow, a land of sun.

26.11.2003
Helsinki

Soccer

I see Kurdistan as a soccer field,
independence as a ball plump with air.
From the beginning of our existence,
running has been our destiny.
This constant motion has been destined: for the ball to fly
and for us to chase it.
Whenever the ball comes to us
we go mad,
and, with all our strength,
we kick it away.

19.4.2004
Helsinki

A Natural-born Lover

My weight is the same weight,
my body is the same body.
Why do I always feel
a woman in my embrace?

5.12.2004
Helsinki

Earth

Soon, we will meet.
Soon, we will merge, like warp and weft.
Then, I will forget all language.
Then, with you,
I will make silence speak.

15.12.2004
Helsinki

Choice

You be the judge:
a wealthy man
to lay down treasure for you to tread on,
a prince
to immediately fulfill
every fancy,
a warrior
who, for your sake, would capture towns and cut off heads,
or a poet
who, with a single word,
brings your body to bloom
and your nipples to tinder.

12.11.2005
Kurdistan

Feet

If not for your feet,
I would have remained in solitude.
On this cold night,
I would have been waiting.

Who says only lips deserve to be kissed?
For Heaven's sake, let my
first kiss land on your toes.

22.11.2006
Istanbul

Twilight

It is twilight.
the peaks are painted
the color of red pomegranates.
Is it possible that, in his hurry to set,
the sun stumbled?

Is it possible that
the sharp ridges
wounded him?

2006
Kurdistan

Recreation

You have spilled
all over me, the world, the universe
    like a glass of wine.
I wish, just once, I could give you shape
    and see you as you are.

In the dark, I can better see.
In the dark, I can better solve riddles.
You are the remiges of stars:
until it is pitch dark
your beams don't reach my roots or branches.

That's why when you enter my lean-to of black basil
there is no need for light, lamps or candles.

I want to take you apart,
cell by cell, atom by atom,
rephrase you as a single body,
and bind you with desire.

14.4.2007
Helsinki

You Can Never Know How Dear You Are

You can never know how dear you are to me.
If you were an orchard,
every day,
before the sun set fire to the hem of the sky,
I would wake early
and come to you on wings.
Gently, handful by handful, I would till your soil.
Sprout by sprout,
leaf by leaf,
I would fill your minutes with light and melodies.

You can never know how dear you are to me.
Were I a sea and you a hill on my shore,
I would gather an army of soft tides
and make a standard from a wisp of cloud,
and from all sides, in ambush,
I would capture and declare you my island.
Every night, wafting dark basil,
I would close your eyes.
Every morning, I would shower sunlight on you
and bathe you in silk breezes
You can never know how dear you are to me.

4.6.2008
Helsinki

An Early Morning Dream

When I looked up, I saw, far off,
a tornado
swerving, tilting, drawing near,
its entire height: light.
An angel faced me.
Her finger rose slowly.
She said, "Good news:
this thin path leads to heaven.
Don't stray from it. Take it and go."
Not to one side did I turn my head.
Not by one hair did I part from the road.
But, the tornado
deafened with great fury,
sweeping me closer toward hell's abyss.
Suddenly
before me
a silver birch appeared.
I embraced her.
Both my arms locked around her.
I held tight until no strength was left in me.
When I woke, my silver birch,
I was drenched in sweat.
My arms were twined around you.

25.1.2010
Helsinki

Graveyard

Why be afraid of the graveyard?
At least in that land,
in that land,
I can settle in a little house of my own
that will let me forget my migration from warren to warren,
a little house
I will never pay rent for,
where no one will ever ask me to return the key.

9.2.2010
Helsinki

After

A choir, an essence,
the room chaotic as judgment day:
on the pillow,
a slim thread, thin, so thin, shines.
Is it the glistening beam of a fallen star
or a single hair my sweet friend left behind?

12.7.2010
Riga

A Little Mirror

Is it possible to see
in a little mirror,
in one instant,
the whole universe?

Is it possible
to reach the moon and sun,
to rearrange the stars,
to be a fish
in the azure sea of the sky?

I believed in miracles
the moment I saw a drop of rain
dangle from one of your eyelashes.

26.9.2010
Helsinki

Omar Khayyam in Flight

A thousand times I have wished to know:
if this sky is
an umbrella,
how long will it remain open?
If it is a sea hung upside down,
when will it flood?

If the sky is
a glass display of stars,
the day may come when
a star,
hardheaded, hotheaded,
straining against his space, will,
    with one elbow,
shatter the glass and
cast the rest down.

14.10.2010
Riga and London

Innate Lover

When I first screamed,
I gulped love into my lungs.
Love
cut the umbilical cord,
gave me my first milk,
wove me swaddling clothes,
and built my world from color.
It was love who
sang me my first lullaby,
gave wings to my mind and caused me to speak.

I am an innate lover.
Believe me,
were I a rock at the side of the road,
love for another rock would pierce me,
or I would fall in love with a neighbor:
the felled log, the puddle, the bush,
a bit of dappled light or a patch of shade.
I am an innate lover.

29.12.2010
Riga

Where Lovers Meet

You kill freedom, my dear.
You make me, unmoved by the ticking of time,
oblivious to existence or nonexistence,
    enslaved in the corner.

You grant freedom, dear.
Of our little room
    you made for me a boundless universe.

5.4.2011
Helsinki

Viagra

There's no need to advertise it.
The whole world knows the blue eyes of Viagra,
the service it does to the right and left,
but it strikes me
that our parliamentarians, when they take it,
get indolent,
go dumb,
even swallowing 1,000 pills
won't help.
Only their hands and pockets can get erect.

25.4.2011
Helsinki

Obstinate

Do you know
why I plant my feet in the arena,
why I don't abandon poetry?
I am waiting for a poet
who promised to come.

The poet who will come
is kneaded into being from
angels of the Medes,[21]
the water from Wan Lake and the soil of Hamrin.[22]
When he rushes in,
he is more boundless than the whirlwind,
more courageous than I,
more worldly than I,
more fearless than Qandil's peak.[23]

The poet who will come,
each breath of his
engraves the boulders.
Each glance
lights a candle
in the dark mud houses.

The poet who will come,
where I shut my mouth—
	he thunders

Where I mumble—
his eyes
throw lightning and spark with flame.

---

[21] From 1000 BC onward, the Medes, a people considered to be ancestors of the Kurds, settled in what would be northwestern Iran and southeast Turkey. They called this area Media.
[22] A mountain on the border of Iraq and south Kurdistan (Iraqi Kurdistan).
[23] Qandil is a mountain in south Kurdistan that has been safe haven for rebellious Kurds over the years: peshmerga and the PKK, for example.

Now, you know
why I plant my feet in the arena,
why I don't abandon poetry.
I am still waiting for a poet
who promised to come.

18.6.2011
Riga

Doors and Windows

Every day,
the windows, one by one, all,
all, one by one, I open the windows.
Every day,
the doors, each
I open, each door,
    the doors, each,
before I travel to the land
where there are no windows to open
and the doors never lie down.

21.6.2011
Riga

Suspicion

Stare at your image,
head to toe,
as long as you like.
Decorate yourself as you like.
The choice is yours.
You are free.
As for me,
suspicion has eaten so much of my heart
there isn't much left to consume.
    My mind circles
this tall, slick, lascivious mirror.
I don't know how to blind it,
so it can't gaze
at your figure ever again.

29.6.2011
Riga and Tallinn

Center of the Universe

Who knows
where the core of this universe,
this boundless, infinite universe, is?
You say whatever you say,
but for me
the core of the universe
is a woman's bellybutton.

29.6.2011
Tallinn and Riga

Yellow and Green[24]

I know a region
that feuds with all yellow
    but the purest gold.
I know a region
that feuds with all green but US dollars.

Autumn 2011
Helsinki

---

[24] South Kurdistan: for approximately the past three decades, there have been two major political parties. The PUK identifies itself with green where the PDK uses yellow. They represent the two factions brought to peace after the Kurdish civil war (1994-1997).

To the Critics

You have asked me relentlessly
where I get my freedom,
you persist, asking
how my tongue, naked and alone,
a leaf of meat, soft and helpless,
how, even now, it could
rip out the curtains of Pharaoh's palace,
how, fearlessly, it could
pass through barbed wire, over a land of thorns.

Which throne or crown backs you, you ask.
Whose pocket were you cut from, you ask.

Go easy.
Let me tell you:
when my poverty is a coffer
                              always full,
when my homelessness
                          is a skyscraper,
when always
across the four seasons
my vineyards of grief
grow so juicy and full,
how, then, is freedom not drawn to me?
how, then, is tenacity not my confidante?

25.11.2011
Helsinki

Prison

I flew over
the convulsing sea.
My wings, bloody, rowed the air like oars.
As far as the eye could see,
nature was rearing up
and the sea
was consumed by a coup d'etat.

I looked down
and suddenly saw you.
Joy overwhelmed me.
I thought you an island
to give me calm, shelter.

When I alighted, I saw
you were not shelter,
but the sweetest prison.

5.1.2012
Riga

The World and I

However old this world gets,
every day
fish lay their eggs,
saplings stretch out their new branches,
birds build their nests,
new vines curl,
delicate, so delicate,
revealing themselves to the sun.

I am like this world of mine:
as I age,
every day,
in the little home of my soul,
a small child opens curious eyes.
He begins to trust his own legs.

Make single line and lose para break above
lay their eggs.
A code is broken.
Buried treasure is discovered.

5.1.2012
Riga

The Moon

This white-orbed swan:
when was it parted from its flock?
Why does it fly to such heights?
How is it fastened there?
Did hunters chase it from the globe
or did love for a star
call it upward?

14.1.2012
Riga

Love

I can hide myself so well
no one can find me,
but I don't know where to go,
whom I should beg for protection.
Even if I hide behind the clouds,
love gallops past and grabs my head.

27.1.2012
Helsinki

The Wave

I have seen waves
withdraw so rapidly from the shore
I thought they would never return.
Yet, time after time,
the waves return, lively, galloping.
Oh, dear God,
how alike we are:
I the wave and women the shore.

31.1.2012
Helsinki

Falling Leaves

Wind and leaves entangle:
some leaves
fall with one quick heart
as a bird descends to peck at grain,
others
slither in the air,
once, twice,
they circle, lazily making their way down.
I don't know
what the wind calculates with these leaves:
my days that have passed
or those that remain.

Autumn 2012
Helsinki

The Tree

I suspect the tree is a better lover than I,
the tree and only the tree.
It embraces the soil and doesn't let go
even if you cut it back
or torch it till its last breath,
it won't fly, won't leave,
won't complain,
or change its heart.
I suspect the tree is a better lover than I,
the tree and only the tree.

12.2.2013
Riga

Egoism

All my life was insurrection.
When I die, don't bury me.
Stretch me over the Earth,
stretch me out
naked like Adam.
For the last time, let me rebel.
Let me refuse custom and tradition
I want
to make my bed the entire Earth,
my comforter the whole sky.

2.4.2013
Riga

Attempts

How many times have I tried to live without you,
to run, alone, unburdened,
to find a homeland
without fences, reins, doors, or walls,
but I am so tame, enslaved,
that without you,
panicked and anxious,
I molt.
Loosed from one cage,
I rush to another.

13.8.2013
Riga

When I First Fell in Love

When I first fell in love,
my heart was white,
the whitest white,
my heart a fistful of the first snow.

When I first fell in love,
my heart was hot,
the hottest heat,
my heart a bright, naked ember.

When I first fell in love,
the world had just started to walk,
the snow and the ember were
in perfect harmony, union.

29.10.2013
Helsinki

Kisses Take Root

One night, I sowed a woman's body with kisses:
the steppes of her forehead,
the banks around the wellspring of her lips,
the fertile soil of her forearms and calves,
the hills and valleys of her neck and breast,
the furrows between her fingers and toes,
the high land and low land of her knee and its hollow.

One midnight, not long ago,
to weave fabric for a new poem, I sat at the loom.
When my little heart was content,
when I finished weaving,
what did I see?
On the paper, the kisses had sprouted
the most splendid garden.

9.11.2013
Helsinki

Poetry and Cement

When reading my poems
do you feel the pulse of my voice?
It beats stronger than the chambers of my heart,
but so what?
It is the era of oil, bullets, and cement.

26.6.2014
Helsinki

The Sea

I don't know why
whenever I consider the sea, each time
it seems
the sky has stripped naked
and thrown down her dress.

8.1.2015
Riga

The Mathematician

Whether I sleep or wake,
whether I ride
or walk slowly across the earth,
the phantom of a lidless eye
counts my every second,
notes my every step.

17.11.2015
Riga

CPSIA information can be obtained
at www.ICGtesting.com
Printed in the USA
FSHW01n1806270618
49811FS

9 781944 700805